#GOALS

SEVEN STEPS TO CREATING AND ACHIEVING YOUR GOALS

ISBN: 9781078470346

Published in the USA by:

Voice of Zion Ministries, Int'l

Tucker, Georgia 30085-0852

ISBN 978-1-078-47034-6

Printed in the United States of America

ACKNOWLEDGEMENTS

I would like to acknowledge and thank God for all the gifts He has entrusted to me and for the Grace to be able to finish another written work. I want to thank my children, for helping me grow into the woman I am today. Thank you to all my supporters, students, and mentees. Thank you lastly, but not in the least, my mother, Phyllis, for always believing in me, praying for me, and being a wonderful example of mother, friend, and guide.

TABLE OF CONTENTS

WHAT ARE GOALS AND WHY SET GOALS?

This is the age of self-discovery and actualization. Many people desire to not only know themselves on a deeper existential level but are striving to live their 'best lives'. You too may desire to have more in your life, discover destiny, who you are - and how exactly you fit into the grand scheme of it all. During this quest for truth, you will find that to discover and live your best life, there are some things you must realize and action to take. But where do you start? Nike says, "Just Do It" – but like millions of other people around the world, you are asking "How"? How do you begin to not only come to a place of realization that you need change, but more importantly, how do you do it?

A *goal*, according to Merriam-Webster Dictionary, "is the end toward which effort is directed; aim." The end or object of your efforts and/or ambition that you envision is a *goal*. Actively engaging in the process of identifying goals as well as creating and implementing a plan to accomplish said goals, is the fuel that motivates and pushes us to accomplish the end we aspire to reach. Like driving across country without a map, without goals, we end up aimlessly wandering through life, dependent upon the signs along the road to help us determine where we are in relation to where we want to be. Just like in driving, we may or may not know how long it will take us to get to our destination, what we will need along the way, how much it will cost us, if the vehicle we are driving will make it, or even why we are headed in the direction we are going. Have you ever found yourself striving to achieve something to later realize it isn't what you really want? Perhaps so many unplanned obstacles, incidences and changes have occurred, that now you do not know where you are going or why you are going?

Setting goals not only helps to clarify what you desire to achieve but gives you a vision and helps to facilitate the planning and execution needed to achieve that goal. It helps to maintain focus, motivation, and is a clear roadmap to where you are going. It also brings a sense of accountability, time, tracking progress, and motivation.

TYPES OF GOALS

Part of determining what your goals are, is understanding the types of goals and how they relate to each other. The three main types of goals are those that are based upon time, focus, and topic. For instance, time goals are goals that are defined by the span of time in which they are to be achieved. Within time goals are categories of immediate, short-term, long-term, and lifetime goals. Focus goals are those things that drive or fuel most of our decisions. For instance, wanting to win a Gold Medal in the Olympics. Every decision made up to the point of competing in the Olympics will be predicated on this one Goal. The decision to train with a world-renowned trainer, waking up at 4 a.m. to work out, watching what you eat, dating or not dating, may all be influenced by this one goal. Lastly, topic-based goals can be either financial, professional or personal. These goals may be ones like, wanting to obtain training in Real Estate to become an agent. Learning financial management for career advancement or saving money for a down payment on a house.

For instance, you may have a topic goal of becoming a Real Estate agent. Through research, you discover that you will need classroom training for a specific number of hours, pass a state exam, find a broker, and pay license fees. This goal can be a short-term goal based upon your readiness and motivation, it can be completed in a few months. A focus goal would be becoming the top agent in your firm, this would be the motivation to take extra training in sales and marketing, it could be the 'why' you possess that causes you to get a mentor, join a networking group, and do open houses to gain more potential clients and sales. It would be a long-term goal, that you would set shorter, more immediate goals to achieve.

We have defined what goals are, there characteristics and types, as well as how they benefit us in helping us to chart a course of success in our everyday lives however, for many, being able to identify or articulate a specific goal is challenging. For instance, having a desire to accomplish a task, is not the same as having clearly defined goals that will charter a course to deliver you the results you desire. Many have ideas and dreams in their head, like I once did, but lack the organization it takes to accomplish what they are dreaming. This is not due to lack of ability to accomplish, but lack of a clear plan. Remember our earlier example? Traveling across country without a map or GPS leaves us wandering around the country, possibly taking a longer route than necessary, and perhaps never reaching our destination.

Setting Meaningful Goals

The first step in goal setting involves brainstorming your goals. Long-term goals are created, then systematically refined.

Desire: What do you really want?

Step 1: Brainstorm: *Write down everything you can think of* (big or small) that you would like to change, achieve or do. This activity is designed for long-term goals that you want to accomplish within 1 year, however you can apply the same process for longer-term goals or shorter-term goals. When working with goals that will take more than 1 year to implement, you will need to identify which aspects of the goal can be tackled in the first year and focus your attention there.

Step 2: Simplify and Prioritize: Look at your list and group items that are similar or that can be combined into one larger goal. Look at your simplified goals and circle the ones you feel are your highest priority. Rate each circled goal on a scale of 1 to 3, 1 being the highest priority and 3 being the least.

Step 3: Identify 1 to 2 major goals for this year (5 or more for Long-term goals): Looking at your priorities, identify 1 to 2 major goals that will make the biggest impact on your life or organization. Always approach the most important goals first. Note that if you are using this process for your organization, you may need to accomplish ALL the goals you have identified. The execution is more complex; however, the same process applies.

DRIVE: Why do you want it?

KNOWING YOUR "WHY" Focus on Outcomes: Look at the goals you've identified and ask yourself the following questions (for each goal):

Major Goal	Why is this desirable?	What is the desired outcome?	What will happen if this goal is not met?

S.M. A². R². T. GOALS

Every successful person agrees, setting goals and achieving them are keys to their success in business, financial planning, family, and personal growth. As previously discussed, goal setting is crucial if you desire to change your life, circumstances, habits, financial position, career, business, or emotional health. More importantly, your goals must be well-defined and focused. One of the most widely used guideline or rules in setting goals is the S.M.A².R².T. goal setting model. S.M. A². R². T. goals comprise of five specific elements that serve as a guideline in constructing precise, obtainable goals: Specific, Measurable, Achievable, Realistic, and Time-bound. I have added two extra components to the S.M.A.R.T. model that I have found to bring even more clarity and success in achieving goals, "action" and "relevance". According to Dr. R. Feenstra (2016), "a goal without *action* is a dream". He further postulates that models that neglect to include *relevance* within them "provide no guidance on how to evaluate multiple goals" (Feenstra, 2016) as they do not consider that we often have more goals than time allows and that some goals are interdependent. As I agree with Dr. Feenstra's evaluation of the S.M.A.R.T. model, I teach the model including the additional criteria of action and relevance. Unlike Dr. Feenstra however, I do not exclude the widely acceptable criteria of *achievable* and *realistic* as both are essential in the planning and setting goals. Both achievability and realistic components serve as foundation qualifications of goals that heavily determines the outcome of successful goal accomplishment for a person or organization. Therefore, the model I teach is better illustrated through the acronym S.M. A². R². T.

Below, we further examine each of the components of the S.M. A². R². T. model:

Specific

The best goals are those that are clearly defined and focused. It is easily identified once you achieve it. Take the time to make sure it is as specific and identifiable as possible. Ask, "Is this goal specific or broad?" If not, think of ways in which it can be more specific. Instead of "I want to be a teacher", make it more precise with, "I want to teach math to middle school students".

Measurable

The ability to ascertain whether you have achieved your goals is imperative. You should without question, be able to know if you have accomplished your goal or how much progress you have made. Measurable goals are ones with targets and have milestones (benchmarks) used to ensure that you are progressing on track and will indicate when you have accomplished your goal. Knowing how to plan to measure your success is an essential part of goal setting.

Measurement of your goals should be both performance base as well as outcome focused. Performance in goal setting relates to both progress and methods used to accomplish goals. For instance, in losing weight, you may implement a certain diet to assist in reaching your goal weight during which you would track daily caloric intake and weight. All are actions or performances by you. Outcomes refer to the goal to lose 10 lbs. The loss of 10 lbs. is the outcome you desire but speaks nothing to the actual performance involved in obtaining the goal weight lost.

Achievable and Actionable

It goes without saying, no one wants to embark on a task knowing that it is likely they won't succeed. Likewise, in setting your goals it will be beneficial to evaluate each one considering your own capabilities or resources. This is not to disqualify those major dreams we sometimes look to achieve, but to initiate an honest evaluation of our current abilities and resources, i.e. access to assistance, information, education, etc. that will help to facilitate the steps or tasks needed to be complete for us to reach our intended goal. For instance, it is okay to have a goal of becoming a teacher, however, if after evaluating your past education and experience along with the requirements to become a certified teacher you discover you don't have all the necessary requirements and education, that goal will not be obtainable to you until those requirements are met. Those requirements can then become sub-goals that you can achieve over time, with every accomplishment getting you closer to your long-term goal of being a teacher. Perhaps you do have the education, but lack certification, in this case certification will be the short-term goal.

The steps you take leading to the accomplishment of your goal is the action or tasks you will complete to realize your goal. Each action or tasks should be something you can do either immediately, or with assistance or additional resources or training.   These steps also serve as a unit of measure or milestone in constructing larger or complex goals. Conversely, having a goal of joining the military and becoming a major in the Army and you are celebrating your 55th birthday would probably not be a goal that is achievable at this time in your life. I am not saying you are not physically able to do the things solders do, however, there is a requirement set by the Military Branch of Government that would prohibit you from joining at a late age and advancing through the ranks.

The ability to be honest and fair in our personal evaluations of our strengths, weaknesses and abilities is foundational in setting successful oriented goals. If we are not realistic with our evaluations and processes in constructing and planning our goals, we will set ourselves up for failure. One of the tools I like to use to evaluate myself is a SWOT Analysis. SWOT analysis

12

looks at your strengths, weaknesses, opportunities, and threats. This tool is widely used by business developers, entrepreneurs, and managers, but is shown to be equally as useful to assess individuals in their personal life decisions.

Please research and use this tool to help you to better construct goals that you are sure to achieve.

Realistic and Relevant

Realistic goals are goals that you have carefully considered the rate of success. How likely are you to achieve this goal? Consider the steps or sub-goals needed to reach the goal. Realistic goals provide motivation and drive needed to achieve your dreams of success in business or in your personal life. Having goals and achieving them builds self-esteem, sense of well-being, and happiness. Therefore, having realistic goals is essential in your overall journey to living your best life, vision, and destiny.

Likewise, relevancy of your goal to your overall mission and/or vision is also imperative. To maximize the outcomes of your goal setting, you want to ensure that your goals align with your values and vision, as well as being most aligned with your long-term goals of success.

Time-bound

Lastly, in setting successful goals that you are sure to achieve, the element of time must be included. Dr. Feenstra (2016) expresses the importance of inclusion of feedback at set intervals of time. These set feedback times act as milestones in which you can assess progress towards your goals and acts as a trigger in which you evaluate your goals. Perhaps at one of these milestones, you discover it more beneficial to adjust your process. For instance, in losing weight, you may discover after three weeks, you have not lost the desired weight on a

13

program and decide that another program that has been proven to yield better results would work best. In business, perhaps you are using a method for advertising, but have found after a month that you have not had an increase in sales. At this point, you may decide to try a different method of advertising or perhaps invest more in your efforts.

It is important to set milestones, as well as giving yourself a set time to determine whether the goal has been achieved or not.

ACHIEVING YOUR GOALS

Creating goals are the beginning of the process of success but without action, it is literally a dream. Now that you understand what a goal is and how to create goals that you can achieve, it is time to create a map or daily plan that will help you to reach your destination. Depending upon whether the goal is a long-term or short-term goal, you will need to write out determined steps or action items you need to take to accomplish the goal you set. For long-term goals, it is best to plan in 60-day increments of actionable items, 30-day planning works for short-term goals, as well as daily planning for both goal types.

These increments of time will become 'milestones' to measure your progress towards your goals. For instance, in business start-ups, an inspiring entrepreneur would have several actionable items in relation to starting the business, one of which would include developing a written business plan, conceptualizing the name of the business, incorporating, etc. Each item would be prioritized as previously explained, and a deadline would-be set-in order to achieve this goal, as in the S.M. A^2. R^2. T model shown to you. Using a planner, white board, or journal, you will need to track your progress. There may be several action items needed to complete your milestone, for instance, the writing of each section of a business plan can be broken out across daily or weekly goals and tracked, once all components are complete, you would have succeeded in completing a milestone toward starting your own business. Another milestone would be incorporating your business which may include several actionable items across weeks, including hiring an attorney, or business professional to help you.

WRAPPING UP

S.M. A^2. R^2. T. goal setting is one of the most widely-used, user friendly methods of setting and achieving goals. Whether long-term goals that span over the next five to ten years, or short-term goals that can be reached within weeks to months, having a tool that can organize, measure and chart out your goals visibly brings great motivation, faith, and confidence that you will succeed. Start today using the S.M. A^2. R^2. T. goal setting model. I have included seven simple steps that will help you plan and achieve success. Also included are worksheets to assist you in understanding and creating your milestones through sub-goal creation, short-term goal planning, monthly planning, and creating a weekly "Ta-da list". A "Ta-da list" is a to-do list that gives a sense of the ease and satisfaction that you will get when you find yourself moving purposely toward your goals. It is a simple as "Ta-da" and its done, when you learn to prioritize your goals on a smaller, more manageable level.

Goals are foundational tools used by some of the most successful and purpose driven people in the world. In our quest for personal, financial, spiritual, and relational successes, nothing will single handedly quantify and assist us like having goals that are achieved through a methodical and clear process. For many, going from an idea to ultimate success can be daunting, stressful, and seem hopeless. Fortunately, now you can confidently say, "I am not afraid to go for the gold!" and realize your dreams, whatever they may be. Dream, brainstorm, write down, and organize your dreams. Plan and execute and achieve your goals with successful goal setting.

Checklist and Worksheets

To get the most out of the workbook, I have provided a 5-step guide along with corresponding worksheets that you can use to create a list of informal ideas and then turn them into structured goals.

Checklist:

☐ Step 1 – Brainstorm – Create a List

☐ Step 2 – Simplify and Prioritize

☐ Step 3 - Pick Your Top 2 (Long-term goals pick 5)

☐ Step 4 – Structure Your Goals

    ☐ a. Specific

    ☐ b. Measurable

    ☐ c. Achievable and Actionable

    ☐ d. Realistic and Relevant

    ☐ e. Time-bound

☐ Step 5 – Outcomes Expected

☐ Step 6 – Final Draft

☐ Step 7 – Achieving Your Goals – Milestones and Planning

Step #1 – Brainstorm - Create a List

Take 30-minutes to create a list of things you would like to either accomplish or experience. This list will make up your current **informal goals**. Structure will be added later. Focus on developing a mental picture of some end state, some outcome, e.g. publish a novel, travel to China, etc. Each item should be no longer than a single sentence. If it helps, you can think of it as creating a "bucket list".

Step #2 – Simplify and Prioritize

At this point in the process, revisit and group similar goals together. Next, prioritize which actions and/or goals are the ones you will be pursuing first, second, third, etc.

_____

_____

_____

_____

_____

_____

Step #3 – Pick Your Top 2 (5 for Long-term Goals)

Using what you have written down in worksheet #1, decide on your top 5 goals. Of all the things on your list, which are the goals you really want to accomplish? You can create a fresh list using the worksheet provided, or you can simply enumerate on your original list. A recommendation is to look towards any bigger, longer-term goals you might have. Remember also to think about what drives you to want to accomplish these goals.

_____

_____

_____

_____

Note: this step is in part selecting which goals you feel are most **Realistic**. You want to select goals you believe will be most relevant i.e., impactful on achieving your biggest dreams or visions.

Step #4 – Structure Your Goals – S.M.A.R.T.

The lists created in step #1 and #2 are still informal goals. Now it is time to use the S.M.A.R.T. format to provide some structure. Take each goal, independently, and fill in the worksheet.

Goal # ____ (_____)

Informal description

#3a Specific – 1st draft

#3b Measurable – remember both outcome and performance measures

#3c Actionable – list at least 3 next actions or sub-goals (milestone achievements). Make sure each sub-goal is achievable, i.e., within your scope of ability or power to accomplish. If not, are there specific sub-goals that will prepare you to accomplish the goal. Perhaps, this goal should be prioritized differently to prepare you to move forward.

#3d Realistic and Relevant – Revisit your goal, ask, are the previous two steps and actions realistic? Is this goal relevant to my long-term goals, do they align with my values, abilities, and dreams? Make any revisions below:

#3e Time Bound – establish by when the goal will be accomplished.

Step #5 – Expected Outcomes

Take each goal and now write an "expected outcome". Each outcome should provide an element to measure your success. Remember to keep in mind some goals may require more than one criterion of measurement and the difference between outcomes versus performance.

Goal #1

Goal #2

Goal #3

Goal #4

Goal #5

Step #6 – Final Draft

You should now have completed two (2) to five (5) worksheets for step 3. Take each goal and now write a formal "goal statement". Each statement should include each component of the SMART model covered in the worksheet.

Goal #1

Goal #2

Goal #3

Goal #4

Goal #5

Step #7 – Achieving Your Goals – Milestones and Planning

In step #2 you have already decided which of your informal goals are most relevant. Now you have at least 5 goals you finalized in step #7. At this point in the process, using only the goals you selected and refined, begin to brainstorm sub-goals for each goal and these are your "milestones". Group the milestones into major milestones and number each one in order of completion.

_____
_____
_____
_____
_____
_____
_____
_____
_____
_____

Milestones:

1.) _____

2.) _____

3.) _____

4.) _____

5.) _____

6.) _____

7.) _____

8.) _____

9.) _____

10.) _____

11.) _____

12.) _____

60-Day Plan.

Now pick only the first two milestones and create a list focusing only on their completion. Research shows that anything planned beyond 60-days is subject to change, so we will only focus on two milestones at a time. Think about the steps you need to take to accomplish these two goals, in order of priority. Write down everything you can think of needed to achieve these two goals, arrange in order of priority and what NEEDS to be done first to move on to the next item, etc.

_____

_____

_____

_____

_____

_____

_____

30-Day Plan.

Take the priority items and make a list for month 1 and put the rest in a list for month 2 and save it for later.

For each monthly sub-goal, brainstorm all the tasks that will need to be done to accomplish each sub-goal in 30-days. Details are essential as each task needs to be executable, leaving nothing out.

_____

_____

_____

_____

_____

_____

Prioritize each task on a scale from 1 to 4, 1 being most important or needs to be done before you can do other tasks, and 4 being least important or time-sensitive.

Now you have your next 4 weeks of tasks (1 through 4). Next, move to making a weekly plan.

Weekly "Ta-Da" list.

Make sure you display and can access your list either using a white board, planner, or spreadsheet.

Looking at your monthly plan, start with the highest priority numbered #1 and identify all tasks needing to be complete in order to accomplish your first prioritized sub-goal. Mark all task in order of importance from 1 through 3 and do number 1 first. Schedule all tasks that are time-sensitive and assign other tasks to specific days.

It is also important to have a daily plan. Schedule time each day for 10 – 15 minutes to plan your next day with items needing to be completed in order of priority.

1. Choose three to five tasks for the day.

2. Determine desired outcomes.

3. Prioritize tasks.

4. Schedule any appointments.

Two Examples of What Your Daily Plan Could Look Like:

Simplified

Today's Tasks (in order of priority)	Notes
1	
2	
3	
4	
5	

Detailed

TASKS	OUTCOMES	NOTES/COMPLETED?
Priority Task 1:		
Priority 2:		
Priority 3:		
Other Tasks:		

www.ingramcontent.com/pod-product-compliance
Lightning Source LLC
Chambersburg PA
CBHW081025170526
45158CB00010B/3157